Reading Comprehension

Written by Shannon Kee

Illustrations by David Coulson

FlashKids

An imprint of Sterling Children's Books

This book belongs to

_____

FLASH KIDS, STERLING, and the distinctive Sterling logo are registered trademarks of
Sterling Publishing Co., Inc.

Published by Sterling Publishing Co., Inc.
387 Park Avenue South, New York, NY 10016
Text and illustrations © 2007 by Flash Kids
Distributed in Canada by Sterling Publishing
c/o Canadian Manda Group, 165 Dufferin Street
Toronto, Ontario, Canada M6K 3H6
Distributed in the United Kingdom by GMC Distribution Services
Castle Place, 166 High Street, Lewes, East Sussex, England BN7 1XU
Distributed in Australia by Capricorn Link (Australia) Pty. Ltd.
P.O. Box 704, Windsor, NSW 2756, Australia

Sterling ISBN 978-1-4114-3476-9

Manufactured in Canada

Lot #:
9 11 13 14 12 10
01/17

For information about custom editions, special sales, premium and
corporate purchases, please contact Sterling Special Sales
Department at 800-805-5489 or specialsales@sterlingpublishing.com.

Cover design and production by Mada Design, Inc.

Dear Parent,

Once young children have learned to read, the next important step is to ensure that they understand and retain the information they encounter. The passages and activities contained in this book will provide your child with plenty of opportunities to develop these vital reading comprehension skills. The more your child reads and responds to literature, the greater the improvement you will see in his or her mastery of reading comprehension. To get the most from *Reading Comprehension*, follow these simple steps:

- Provide a comfortable and quiet place for your child to work.
- Encourage your child to work at his or her own pace.
- Help your child with the problems if he or she needs it.
- Offer lots of praise and support.
- Encourage your child to work independently to gain confidence in his or her problem solving skills.
- Allow your child to enjoy the fun actvities in this book.
- Most of all, remember that learning should be fun!

Visit us at *www.flashkidsbooks.com* for free downloads, informative articles, and valuable parent resources!

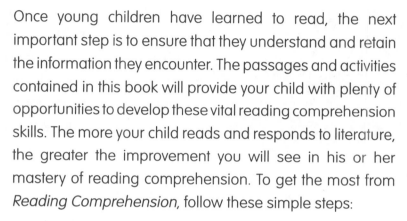

Phillis Wheatley

In the late 1700s, most slaves were not allowed to read or write. During this time there was one black slave who not only wrote poems, but published them too! Her name was Phillis Wheatley, and she was the first African-American poet.

Phillis was born in Senegal, Africa. At the age of seven she was kidnapped by slave traders. A ship brought her to Boston, where John and Susannah Wheatley purchased her. The Wheatleys treated Phillis more like a member of the family than a slave. They saw Phillis writing on the wall with chalk one day, but they didn't punish her. Instead, they helped her learn to read and write. By the time Phillis was twelve, she could read Greek, Latin, and verses from the Bible.

Phillis started writing poetry when she was only thirteen years old. Her first poem was published in 1767 in the *Newport Mercury* newspaper. When a preacher in Boston died in 1770, Phillis wrote a poem about him. Many people in Boston liked her poem, and Phillis became well-known. A few years later, a book with 39 of Phillis's poems was published in London. It was the first book published by an African-American.

In 1776, Phillis wrote a poem to George Washington and mailed it to him. Washington thought Phillis was very talented, and he invited her to meet him. When the Wheatleys passed away, Phillis became a free woman. She used her talent with words to write an antislavery letter, which she also sent to George Washington.

Phillis married a free black man in 1778, and she moved away from Boston. She wrote more poems, but her fame declined. She had an unhappy marriage and eventually moved back to Boston, where she passed away. After her death, people continued to publish her poems and letters. Today people still study and read her writings.

Find your way through the maze by connecting the events in the correct sequence.

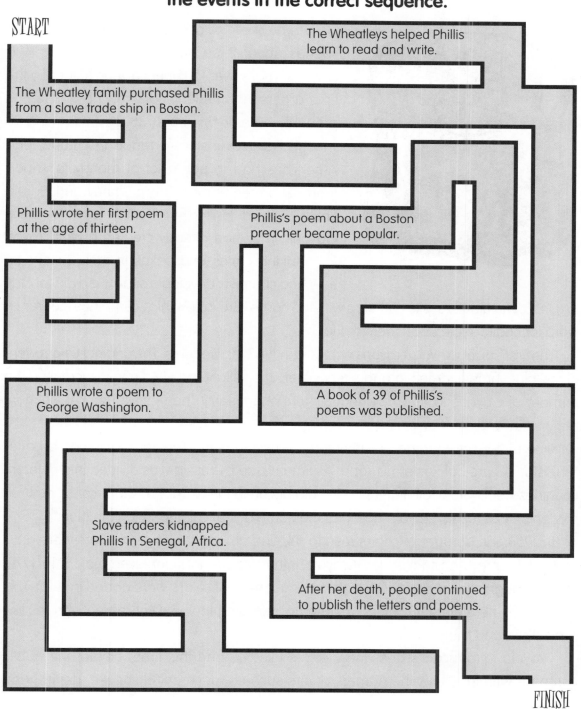

START

The Wheatleys helped Phillis learn to read and write.

The Wheatley family purchased Phillis from a slave trade ship in Boston.

Phillis wrote her first poem at the age of thirteen.

Phillis's poem about a Boston preacher became popular.

Phillis wrote a poem to George Washington.

A book of 39 of Phillis's poems was published.

Slave traders kidnapped Phillis in Senegal, Africa.

After her death, people continued to publish the letters and poems.

FINISH

What Color Is Your Crayon?

Do you like to color? The average American kid spends about three hours a week coloring with crayons. That's over 150 hours a year! In fact, by the time a person turns ten years old, he or she has probably worn down about 730 crayons.

The first crayons were made in Europe, and Americans had to pay a lot of money to import them. Two men named Edwin Binney and Harold Smith wanted to find a cheaper way to make crayons. They had already created a wax crayon for marking crates and boxes in their factory. So they had chemists develop a similar crayon for kids to use. Edwin Binney's wife came up with the name "Crayola," which combines the French word for chalk, "craie," with the word for oil.

The first box of Crayola crayons was sold in 1903 for five cents. The original colors were black, blue, brown, green, orange, red, violet, and yellow. In 1949, Crayola increased the number of crayons to 48. They added more shades with names like apricot, salmon, periwinkle, and cornflower.

One of the colors added in 1949 was "Prussian Blue." The color was named after "Prussia," an area of Eastern Europe. As time passed, Prussia was divided into different countries. Teachers wrote letters to Crayola because the word "Prussian" confused their students. As a result, Crayola changed the name of that color to "midnight blue."

In 1958, the number of colors rose to 64, and among the 16 new colors were navy blue, goldenrod, and lavender. Crayola introduced eight fluorescent colors in 1972, which brought the total up to 72. Eight more fluorescent colors were added in 1990. This meant that there were 80 colors at this time, including the new fluorescent shades like radical red and magic mint.

Crayola introduced sixteen new colors in 1993, and this time they let the public come up with ideas for the names. Colors such as macaroni & cheese, denim, and shamrock were added to bring the total number of colors up to 96. In 1998, that number jumped from 96 to 120 with shades including cotton candy and outer space.

Crayola started out with a small box of eight crayons, and now both the company and the crayon boxes are much bigger. Every year they produce about three million crayons. They now sell their crayons in 80 different countries and twelve languages!

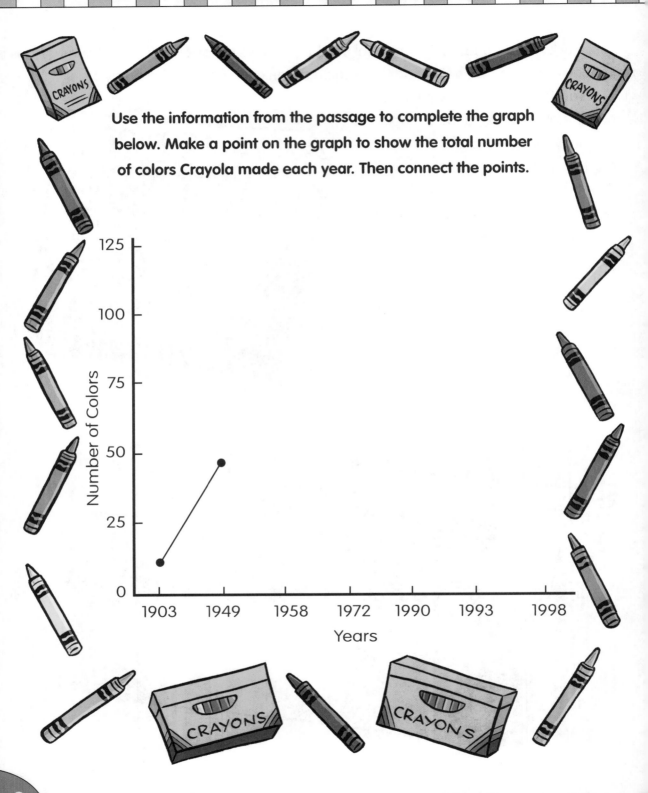

Use the information from the passage to complete the graph below. Make a point on the graph to show the total number of colors Crayola made each year. Then connect the points.

Number of Colors

125

100

75

50

25

0

1903   1949   1958   1972   1990   1993   1998

Years

8

> A **conclusion** is something not stated in the passage. You draw conclusions using clues from the text and your own logic.

1. Circle the most logical conclusion you can draw from the passage.

   a) Crayola crayons were popular and sold well. People liked having lots of color choices and wanted more new colors.

   b) Nobody was buying Crayola crayons because they were too messy.

   c) The crayons were too expensive because there were so many colors. Crayola will never add any more new colors.

2. Read the conclusion and circle the clues that support it. There may be more than one correct clue!

   Conclusion: Crayola listens to what the public thinks about their crayons.

   Clues:

   a) Since their company started, Crayola has made 100 billion crayons.

   b) When teachers wrote letters to Crayola, they changed a color name from "Prussian blue" to "midnight blue."

   c) The eight original colors were yellow, red, orange, green, blue, violet, brown, and black.

   d) In 1993, Crayola asked the public to help name sixteen new crayon colors.

3. Find clues from the reading passage that support the conclusion. List the facts on the lines below.

   Conclusion: Coloring is a popular activity that lots of kids enjoy.

   Clues: _____

   _____

   _____

   _____

   _____

   _____

Catching the Fog

For most of us, fog is a type of weather. But for some people, fog is a source of water! In places where there isn't enough fresh water, people can collect the fog and turn it into water. How does all this work?

If you've ever walked through a patch of fog, you might have noticed that your skin and hair felt damp. This is because fog is actually made of tiny water droplets. Scientists are helping people collect these droplets to make drinking water. Often, these people live in towns where there is no fresh water source. They rely on trucks to deliver fresh water, which is expensive. It's better for a town to be able to make its own fresh water.

People have always looked to rain as a source of fresh water. Since rain falls toward the ground, it can easily be collected into tanks. But the water droplets that make up fog don't hit the ground. Instead, they float in the air. Fog is a lot like a cloud that hovers close to the ground. To turn fog into water, you have to catch the water droplets.

A fog catcher is made of nets stretched between two posts. Usually the nets are set up on a hilltop or in a valley where fog often settles. As fog drifts by, the nets trap the water droplets. Beads of water run down the nets and collect into gutters. The gutters and pipes guide the water into large tanks where it can be stored. A fog catcher can collect up to 10,000 liters of water a day. Scientists have helped set up fog catchers for towns in Chile, Nepal, and Mexico.

Fog catchers are a great way for people in isolated towns to have their own fresh water source. Centuries before scientists created fog-catching nets, nature was making fog into water on its own. As fog passed through the mountains, large leaves trapped the droplets just like the nets do. Native people learned to drink the tiny pools of water that collected on the leaves. Thanks to modern fog catchers, enough water can be made to supply a whole town!

Read each sentence and check whether it gives the main idea of the passage or a supporting detail.

	Main Idea	Supporting Detail
1. Fog is a lot like a cloud that hovers close to the ground.		
2. A fog catcher can collect up to 10,000 liters of water a day.		
3. Fog catchers are a great way for people in isolated towns to have their own fresh water source.		
4. A fog catcher is made of nets stretched between two posts.		
5. Scientists have helped set up fog catchers for towns in Chile, Nepal, and Mexico.		
6. Native people learned to drink the tiny pools of water that collected on the leaves.		
7. In places where there isn't enough fresh water, people can collect the fog and turn it into water.		
8. Thanks to modern fog catchers, enough water can be made to supply a whole town!		

Puppy Raising

Gabe had been begging his father for a dog for months. But when his dad came home one day with a Golden Retriever puppy, Gabe was in for a big surprise.

"This is Tracer, and he's a very special dog," Gabe's dad explained. "We're going to help raise this puppy to become a guide dog."

"You mean the kind of dog that helps blind people?" Gabe asked.

"Exactly," said his dad. "Before Tracer can be a guide dog, he needs to develop social skills. He'll live with us for many months, and then he'll go back to the training school. They will match him with a blind person to be his owner."

"This is the worst idea ever!" Gabe shouted. "I don't want a dog I'll just have to give away!" Gabe stormed off to his room.

At first, Gabe avoided Tracer. Tracer wore a special vest that explained he was a guide dog in training. When Tracer was working, people were not supposed to pet him or play with him. But Tracer also had time to play, and Gabe couldn't resist playing with him. When Tracer got to be bigger, he went to shops and restaurants with Gabe and his dad. They taught him to be confident and friendly, but not to seek attention. Gabe and his dad also taught Tracer voice commands like "sit" and "stay." Gabe enjoyed watching Tracer learn so much.

Months passed, and it was time for Tracer to go back to the school. When Gabe had to say goodbye to Tracer, he felt angry again. It seemed so unfair.

Tracer finished his training at the school, and he was leaving to live with a blind person. Gabe and his dad were invited to the school to meet Tracer's new owner. As they drove to the school Gabe was upset that Tracer was going to live with someone else. After all, they had raised him!

As soon as Gabe saw Tracer with his new owner, his feelings changed. He was proud to see Tracer dressed in a new guide vest, ready for his new owner.

"Thank you for giving Tracer such a good home," the owner said. "In helping to raise Tracer, you've helped me as well."

Gabe was sad to say goodbye to Tracer, but he wasn't angry anymore. He knew that Tracer was going to a good home where he was needed. The owner even told Gabe that he could visit Tracer whenever he wanted.

On the drive home, Gabe was the one who had a surprise for his dad.

"I think we should raise another puppy to become a guide dog!" Gabe said.

Decide if the sentence describes the story's setting, conflict, resolution, or theme. Connect each sentence with the correct word.

1. Gabe meets Tracer's new owner and realizes he is going to a good home.

2. The story takes place at Gabe's home and at the dog training school.

3. Gabe is upset that they will have to give Tracer away after helping train him.

4. Giving away something you love is hard, but helping others makes the sacrifice worth it.

Setting

Conflict

Resolution

Theme

Summarize the plot of the story.

_____

_____

_____

_____

_____

_____

_____

_____

Answer the questions.

1. Why did Gabe storm off to his room when his dad first brought Tracer home?

   _____

   _____

2. What did Gabe and his dad teach Tracer?

   _____

   _____

3. How did Gabe feel on the way to the dog school?

   _____

   _____

4. How did Gabe feel after meeting Tracer's new owner?

   _____

   _____

5. What did Tracer's owner tell Gabe when they met?

   _____

   _____

6. Why did Gabe's feelings change at the end of the story?

   _____

   _____

7. Why do you think Gabe's dad wanted them to be puppy trainers?

   _____

   _____

8. Would you want to be a puppy trainer? What are the good things and bad things?

   _____

   _____

The Hot Dog and the Bun

As you read the passage, look for the underlined sentences. If the statement is a fact, write an F in the box. If it's an opinion, write an O.

1.☐ <u>On a warm summer day, there's nothing better than firing up the grill and cooking some tasty hot dogs.</u> In fact, each summer Americans eat about 7 billion hot dogs. Many of these hot dogs are eaten at summer baseball games. 2.☐ <u>During each baseball season, fans eat about 26 million hot dogs.</u> Babe Ruth once ate so many hot dogs at a baseball game he had to go to the hospital! 3.☐ <u>The best time to have a hot dog is during the month of July, which is National Hot Dog Month.</u>

Americans tend to eat more hot dogs in the summer, but hot dogs are actually popular year-round. Their popularity has made them an American symbol. 4.☐ <u>When King George VI visited the United States from England, he asked to try an American food.</u> So President Roosevelt served him a hot dog. 5.☐ <u>After all, nothing is more American than a hot dog!</u> Or is it?

The idea for the hot dog actually started in Germany, where sausage was popular. 6.☐ <u>In German, the sausage is called a *dachshund*, which means "little dog."</u> When Germans moved to the United States, they brought their "little dogs" with them. Some say that Germans put hot sausages inside milk buns and sold them from carts in New York City. Other people say that the idea for the bun started somewhere else.

The idea for the bun might have come from a man named Charles Feltman. 7.☐ Feltman started out selling pies from his pie cart to Coney Island bars. He came up with the idea of selling sausages on warm rolls, since he could easily prepare them in his cart. 8.☐ Feltman's "Coney Island Hot Dogs" became very popular and he opened his own restaurants.

Other people say the bun idea came from a man named Anton Feuchtwanger. According to the story, Anton was selling hot sausages at a big fair in St. Louis. The sausages were too hot to hold, so Anton loaned people white gloves. When nobody returned the gloves, Anton asked his brother-in-law for help. He was a baker, and he came up with the idea for long rolls to hold the hot meat. 9.☐ This is an unlikely story, so it's probably not true.

Did the idea for the bun come from Germans, Charles Feltman, or Anton Feuchtwanger? Nobody knows for sure. 10.☐ We do know that Americans eat lots of hot dogs—the average American eats 60 a year!

Sleeping Feet

Ouch! Your foot tingles and it feels like you're walking on pins and needles. Somebody tells you that your foot has "fallen asleep." How can your foot be asleep while you're still awake? What causes that tingling feeling?

It all starts with your body's nervous system. There are millions of tiny nerves throughout your body. Imagine a highway filled with cars driving in a loop. Signals from your nerves are like cars: they travel up to the brain to give a message, then they return to the body part with a message from the brain. If a large tree suddenly fell across the highway, what would happen? The cars would be blocked! They couldn't get up to the brain or back to the body parts.

This is what happens when your foot "falls asleep." When you sit on your foot or sleep on your arm, you put pressure on your body part. Too much pressure is like that tree in the road. It blocks the pathway from the body part to the brain. The nerves can't send their messages to the brain.

What happens when a tree blocks a road? A siren rings in the distance, warning drivers that there is danger. A truck races to the spot, removes the tree, and the cars can flow again. When communication between nerves and the brain stops, your body sends out an alarm too. The tingling you feel in your body part is that alarm. It's telling you to change your body position and lift the pressure off the body part that tingles.

Listening to your body's alarm is important. If you let that pathway remain blocked for several hours, it can cause permanent damage to your nerves. The tingling is your body's way of warning you. Because it hurts, it prompts you to change your body position.

As you start to move around, it feels like you're walking on pins and needles. That feeling is your nerves "waking up" and starting to flow. With time the nerves return to normal, and the tingling slowly fades. Pretty soon, your nerves are back on the road, and the highway to your brain is buzzing with new messages.

Find your way through the maze by connecting the events in the correct sequence.

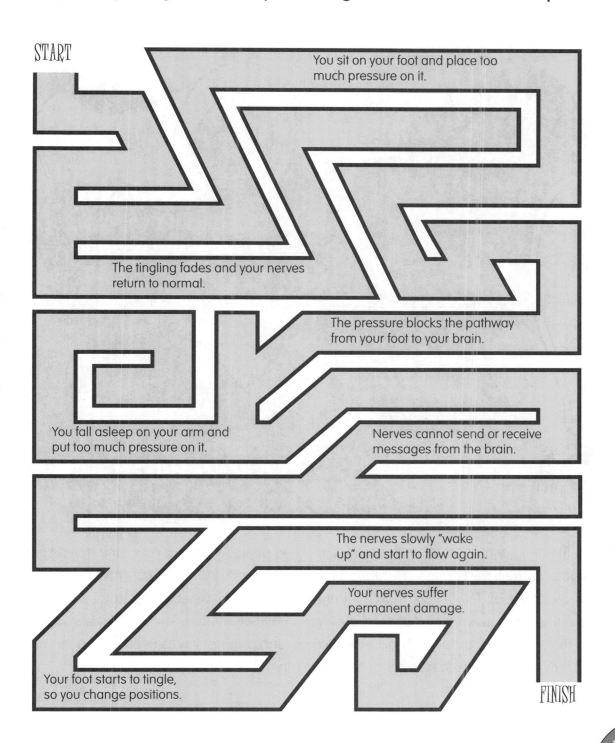

START

You sit on your foot and place too much pressure on it.

The tingling fades and your nerves return to normal.

The pressure blocks the pathway from your foot to your brain.

You fall asleep on your arm and put too much pressure on it.

Nerves cannot send or receive messages from the brain.

The nerves slowly "wake up" and start to flow again.

Your nerves suffer permanent damage.

Your foot starts to tingle, so you change positions.

FINISH

Wagons Going West

Traveling across the country today is fast and easy. Airplanes, cars, and trains carry people to their destinations in hours or days. But back in the 1800s, traveling across the country took four to six months. Ranchers, farmers, miners, and traders traveled westward to make new lives for themselves in unsettled land. These pioneers walked ten to fifteen miles a day, over hills, mountains, and prairies. It was a long, hard journey, but they had wagons to help them make the trip.

The Conestoga was a type of wagon used on many of these journeys. There were three main parts to the wagon: the wagon box, the cover, and the undercarriage. The wagon box was like a long boat. The floor sloped in the middle, which kept barrels from falling out if the wagon went uphill or downhill. The side boards slanted outward to help keep water out.

The wagon cover was called the "bonnet." The bonnet protected the wagon's contents from rain and wind. The bonnet was held up by large wooden bows. Planks of wood were soaked in water until they became bendable. Then they were bent into a U-shape and allowed to dry. The bonnet was stretched over the wooden bows, making a roof for the wagon.

The undercarriage included the wheels and running gear. There were four round iron tires with a hub in the middle of each one. A long piece of wood called a "tongue" stretched out from the front of the wagon. At the end of the tongue was a handle called a "yoke." Pushing forward on the yoke moved the wagon forward. Powerful teams of oxen or mules hauled the heavy loads.

The Conestoga was favored by traders along the Santa Fe Trail, a famous route from Missouri to New Mexico. They liked using the Conestoga because it was large and durable. It could haul up to six tons. Settlers traveling all the way to Oregon and California tried the Conestoga, but it was too big and heavy. Even the strongest oxen could not complete the journey pulling a Conestoga. So, a smaller wagon called a prairie schooner was made. It had the same design as the Conestoga, but was half the size. Families filled the prairie schooners with their food and belongings, and then walked alongside.

Whether by Conestoga or prairie schooner, people relied on their wagons to travel west. Wagons helped shape history as they made it possible for people to make this journey.

Use the information from the passage to complete the diagram below. Label the parts of the wagon using the words in the word box.

wagon box	tire	bow
hub	tongue	yoke
	bonnet	

1. Circle the most logical conclusion you can draw from the passage.
   a) The Conestoga wagon was better than the prairie schooner because it
      was bigger.
   b) It took too long for the wagons to travel long distances, so people should
      have waited until the train was invented.
   c) In the 1800s, wagons were well-designed marvels that made western
      travel possible.

2. Read the conclusion and circle the clues that support it. There may be more than
   one correct clue!
   **Conclusion: The trail to Oregon and California was longer and more difficult
   than the Santa Fe trail.**
   Clues:
   a) Oxen could not complete the journey to Oregon pulling a Conestoga
      wagon.
   b) Wood was soaked in water until it was bendable, then made into bows.
   c) In Santa Fe, Mexicans traded goods with people from Missouri.
   d) People needed smaller wagons called "prairie schooners" to travel to
      California and Oregon.

3. Find clues from the reading passage that support the conclusion. List the facts on
   the lines below.
   **Conclusion: The design of the wagon helped
   settlers overcome obstacles on the trail.**
   Clues: _____

   _____

   _____

   _____

   _____

The Hero's Journey

When we say the word "hero," we are usually talking about someone we admire. We might look up to a hero because he or she did something brave or important. We also come across heroes in the stories we read. Often, a story will tell about a hero who goes on a journey. Many different stories from around the world are about a hero's journey. In each story, the hero seems to follow the same pattern.

Usually, the story begins with the hero being sent on a journey. There is an important task that the hero must complete on this journey, but he's not alone. The hero meets other characters who help him find his way and stay out of danger. At the end of the journey, the hero usually faces a villain and must pass a test. Once he passes the test, the hero is rewarded.

There are lots of stories that follow this same pattern. "Jack and the Beanstalk" is a good example. Jack goes on a journey up the strange beanstalk that grew from the magic beans. He gets help from a fairy and also from the giant's wife. At the end of the story, Jack must face the giant and cut down the beanstalk. Jack and his mother live happily ever after.

Movies sometimes follow this pattern. In "The Wizard of Oz," Dorothy goes on a journey to the land of Oz. She meets the scarecrow, the tin man, and the lion, who help her find her way to the wizard and stay out of danger. The wizard tests Dorothy by making her face the wicked witch. At the end of the story, Dorothy gets to return home.

It's interesting to compare different stories and see how they follow the same pattern of events. The hero's journey can be found in fairy tales, folktales, myths, legends, and even movies. Of course, not all stories about heroes follow this same pattern. Heroes come in all shapes and sizes. Even so, knowing about the hero's journey is helpful. When you read a story that follows the pattern, you can appreciate it even more.

Read each sentence and check whether it gives the main idea of the passage or a supporting detail.

	Main Idea	Supporting Detail
1. The hero is usually sent on a journey with a specific task.		
2. "Jack and the Beanstalk" is an example of the hero's journey.		
3. Stories from around the world follow the pattern of the hero's journey.		
4. The hero usually meets friends who help him on his journey.		
5. Myths, folktales, legends, and even movies tell the story of the hero's journey.		
6. You can compare many different stories about heroes and find the same pattern of events.		
7. The scarecrow, lion, and tin man help Dorothy find her way to the wizard.		
8. At the end of the story, the hero must face the villain and pass a test.		

Prince Sadaka

The African people have a folktale about a Swahili sultan and his son, Prince Sadaka. The sultan had seven sons, and all but Sadaka had left home to travel the world. The sultan missed his sons, but he was too old to go look for them himself. So Prince Sadaka courageously set out on a journey to find his brothers.

Weeks passed as Sadaka sailed across the Indian Ocean. Sadaka was not good at reading maps, and he got lost many times. But he was adventurous and kind, so he made many friends along the way.

Sadaka landed on an island and met some hungry birds. He gave them food, and the birds helped Sadaka sort through his maps. On the next island, Sadaka fed barleycorn to hungry crickets, and they shared their gossip. They had heard rumors about his brothers, and they directed Sadaka to the island of the djinns. The djinns were lonely spirits who frightened most people, but Prince Sadaka spent hours talking with them. In return, they told Sadaka that he could find his brothers on the island of Pemba. Sadaka knew that the sultan of Pemba was a tricky man, so he would have to be careful.

The sultan of Pemba agreed to help Sadaka find his brothers if he could pass three tests. For the first test, Sadaka had to sort three huge bags of seeds before sunrise. Sadaka whistled out to his friends the birds. Just as they had helped him sort his maps, they helped him sort the seeds.

When the sultan came back in the morning, he was impressed that the seeds were all sorted. He gave Sadaka his second test, which was to cut down a giant tree with one stroke of his sword. This time, Sadaka asked the djinns for help. The djinns hollowed out the tree, so Sadaka could easily cut it down with one stroke of his sword.

For the third test the sultan brought Sadaka to a ball at the palace. He told Sadaka to find his favorite daughter and dance with her. This time, Sadaka called on the chattering crickets for help. The crickets whispered in Sadaka's ear and helped him find the sultan's favorite daughter. As Sadaka danced with her, the sultan was very pleased.

The sultan told Sadaka what had happened to his brothers. When they came to Pemba, they had been very rude, so he put them into his dungeon. Because Sadaka passed the three tests, the sultan let the brothers go free. And the sultan's daughter thought Sadaka was so clever, she agreed to marry him.

Decide if the sentence describes the story's setting, conflict, resolution, or theme.

Connect each sentence with the correct word.

1. The story takes place in Africa and on the island of Pemba.

2. Prince Sadaka makes friends who help him find his way and pass the three tests.

3. If you are generous to those you meet, they will help you in your time of need.

4. Sadaka gets lost while searching for his brothers, and then he faces three difficult tests.

Setting

Conflict

Resolution

Theme

Summarize the plot of the story.

_____

_____

_____

_____

_____

_____

_____

_____

_____

Answer the questions.

1. Why did Prince Sadaka go on a journey to find his brothers?

   _____

   _____

2. Why did Sadaka get lost as he sailed?

   _____

   _____

3. What three friends did Sadaka make as he searched for his brothers?

   _____

   _____

4. How did each friend help Sadaka find his brothers?

   _____

   _____

5. What three tests did the sultan of Pemba give Sadaka?

   _____

   _____

6. How did Sadaka's friends help him pass the tests?

   _____

   _____

7. Why had the sultan of Pemba put the brothers in jail?

   _____

   _____

8. Do you think Sadaka's story follows the pattern of the hero's journey?

   _____

   _____

Colonial Careers

As you read the passage, look for the underlined sentences. If the statement is a fact, write an F in the box. If it's an opinion, write an O.

Colonial towns buzzed with activity from sunrise to sunset. There was always work to be done, and colonial people believed that laziness was a sin. Even children were expected to get up early and do chores. 1.☐ <u>When a boy turned nine years old, he became an apprentice, or assistant.</u> This is where he learned how to do one of the jobs in a colonial town. What were some of these job choices?

A cooper was important to the town because he worked with wood. A cooper fixed chairs, built barrels and tubs, and made wagon wheels. 2.☐ <u>The miller, on the other hand, had a much more boring job.</u> He ran the mill that ground grain for farmers. The farmers didn't pay the miller with money. Instead, the miller kept a portion of the grain as payment.

3.☐ <u>The blacksmith had the most interesting job in the town.</u> The blacksmith made things with iron, like horseshoes, pots, and nails. Farmers depended on blacksmiths to make hoes, plows, and axes. Sometimes the blacksmith was a dentist because he had the right tools for pulling teeth out. 4.☐ <u>Pulling people's teeth would be a terrible part of the job, especially during colonial times.</u>

The silversmith had a similar job as the blacksmith, but worked with silver instead of iron. 5.☐ <u>Unlike most other colonial jobs, a woman could be a silversmith.</u> A silversmith made dinner dishes and silverware. Some people might buy plates from a pewterer instead of the silversmith. Pewter was more expensive than silver, so most colonists could not afford it. 6.☐ The pewterer's job was not very important since only wealthy people could buy pewter.

Colonial towns also had cobblers for making shoes. During this time the shoes were not fancy. In fact, the cobbler used the same pattern for every shoe, so the left and right shoes were exactly the same! 7.☐ Those shoes must have looked really strange. While the cobblers made shoes, tailors and tanners made clothes. 8.☐ The tailor used cloth and the tanner made clothes from animal skins. Tanners also made leather saddles and buckets. 9.☐ Working with leather seems very difficult, so being a tailor would be a better job.

Colonial kids had some interesting choices for careers. 10.☐ They usually worked as apprentices for about seven years to learn their job. Most colonial people did the same job their whole life. It gave them the chance to perfect their craft. The better each person was at doing their job, the more useful they were to the town!

The Man with a Million Stories

Have you ever played the game "Marco Polo" in the pool? One swimmer closes his eyes and yells "Marco," and the other swimmers shout "Polo" in reply. With his eyes tightly shut, the swimmer explores the unknown water before him, following the sound of their voices. The game is named after a real explorer named Marco Polo, who also explored the unknown.

Born in Venice, Italy, Marco came from a family of traders and merchants. In fact, his father and uncle had left on a journey before Marco was born, and they did not return until he was fourteen years old! When the Polos left on their next trip, Marco went with them. The year was 1271, and Marco was 17 years old.

By 1275, the Polos reached China. They were welcomed by Kublai Khan, the leader of China at that time. Marco spent seventeen years exploring China and had many adventures. In 1295, the Polos finally returned to Venice. Marco was now 41 years old, and he had been gone for 24 years. Marco loved telling stories about the incredible

things he had seen on his travels. The people of Venice called him *il milione* or *Marco milione*, for it was said that he had a million stories to tell.

Later, when Venice was at war with Genoa, Marco Polo was imprisoned. He passed the time in prison by telling stories about his adventures in China. There was another prisoner who started writing down all of Marco's stories. When they got out of prison, the stories of Marco's travels were published. The books inspired many other people to travel and explore. Even Christopher Columbus had a copy of Marco Polo's stories when he sailed to America.

Many people did not believe Marco Polo when he talked about his journey. They thought that he was making it all up. Even today, historians question his information. They argue that Marco's descriptions of China were not accurate, so he must have either made it up or been mistaken about where he was. But Marco Polo always defended his tales. Before he died he said, "I didn't tell half of what I saw."

Find your way through the maze by connecting the events in the correct sequence.

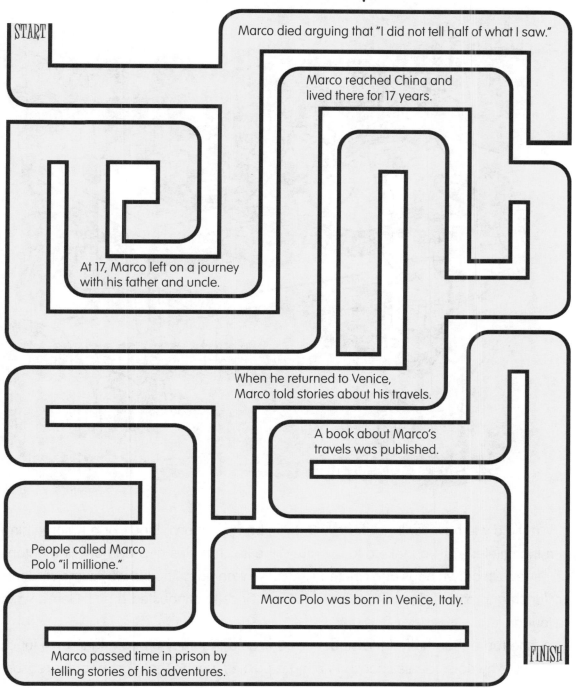

START

Marco died arguing that "I did not tell half of what I saw."

Marco reached China and lived there for 17 years.

At 17, Marco left on a journey with his father and uncle.

When he returned to Venice, Marco told stories about his travels.

A book about Marco's travels was published.

People called Marco Polo "il millione."

Marco Polo was born in Venice, Italy.

Marco passed time in prison by telling stories of his adventures.

FINISH

To Buy or to Bring?

What did you have for lunch today? Did you bring your own lunch, or buy something from the cafeteria? If you take a look around the lunch tables at Longmont Elementary, you'll see both brown bags and cafeteria trays. We wanted to find out why some students buy lunch and others bring it. So the Longmont Gazette conducted a poll. Here's what we found.

A little more than half of the students, 60%, said that they brought their own lunch to school. Why do students choose to bring a packed lunch? The most popular reason, given by 45% of the students, is that they did not like the cafeteria food. "The cafeteria food does not taste good," said Ashley Jensen, "so I bring my lunch." Students who cited this reason described cafeteria food as "bland" and "mushy."

Another 35% of the students said they bring a lunch because they have food allergies. They need to know exactly what they are eating, so they pack their own lunch. The final 20% of the students bring their own lunch because it's faster. "I don't have to wait in the line, and I can start eating my lunch right away," fifth-grader Greg Johnston explained. Karen Green agreed with Greg: "Bringing lunch means you can eat faster and have more time to play."

Many students complain about cafeteria food, but 40% of Longmont students choose to buy food there. What are their reasons? A whopping 50% of the students said the cafeteria gives you more choices. "If you bring your lunch from home you are limited," said Robin Olson. At the cafeteria you can buy hot food like pizza or a cold drink like milk. It tastes better!" Katie Calvin pointed out that a sack lunch "sits in a bag all morning" but cafeteria food tastes "fresh."

The next reason given by 40% of the students who buy lunch is that it's easier. As Andrew Gibbons explains, "If I want to bring lunch, I have to pack it myself. Buying lunch at school is easier, and the food is just as good." Many students said that it was easier to carry money to school to buy lunch than to carry a heavy lunch. Finally, 10% of the students buy lunch to be with their friends. "I'd rather buy lunch and hang out with my friends in line than wait at the table for a long time," said Susan Madsen.

Whether you buy lunch or bring it, the important thing is to eat something healthy and enjoy your lunch break!

Use the information from the passage to label the percentages on the pie chart below.

It's faster

_____

Don't like cafeteria food.

_____

Allergies

_____

Be with friends

_____

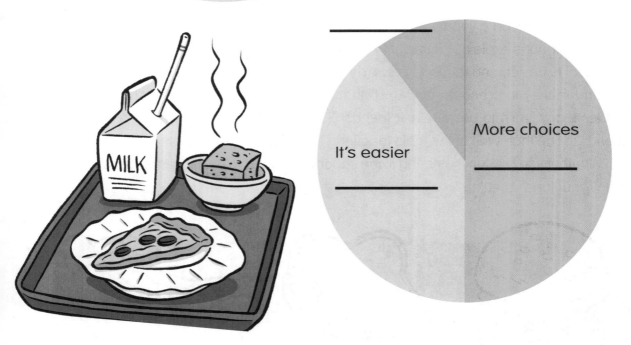

It's easier

_____

More choices

_____

A **conclusion** is something that is not stated in the passage. You draw conclusions using clues from the text and your own logic.

1. Circle the most logical conclusion you can draw from the passage.
    a) Students who bring lunch are smarter than students who buy lunch.
    b) There are advantages and disadvantages to both buying and bringing lunch.
    c) The Longmont cafeteria needs to offer more food choices and have fresher food.

2. Read the conclusion and circle the clues that support it. There may be more than one correct clue!
    Conclusion: Buying food at the cafeteria might take a long time.
    Clues:
    a) Students with allergies prefer to bring lunch rather than buy at the cafeteria.
    b) Cafeteria food tastes fresher than food kept in a bag until lunch time.
    c) Students said they bring their lunch because it's faster than waiting in line.
    d) Susan Madsen said her friends take a long time to buy their lunches.

3. Find clues from the reading passage that support the conclusion. List the facts on the lines below.
    Conclusion: Students disagree about the taste of the cafeteria food.
    Clues: _____

    _____

    _____

    _____

    _____

Animal Astronauts

The first living thing to orbit Earth in a spaceship was not a human. It was a dog! The dog's name was Laika, and the Soviet Union sent her into space in 1957. As Laika floated in orbit, scientists monitored her heart rate, breathing, and blood pressure. They were able to learn about the effects of space travel on living things. Laika was only one of many animals who traveled in space, paving the way for human astronauts.

While the Soviets were sending dogs into space, the United States was sending monkeys. In 1952, the United States sent two monkeys named Patricia and Mike into space. Scientists wanted to see what would happen when the spaceship accelerated to 2,000 miles per hour. As the spaceship flew to an altitude of 36 miles, scientists watched the monkeys on a video signal. Thanks to Patricia and Mike, they leaned that living things could survive the trip into space. Patricia and Mike landed safely and went to live at the National Zoological Park in Washington, D.C.

Two more monkeys named Able and Baker were launched into space in 1959. This time, the spaceship went much higher and much faster. They flew 300 miles high and traveled over 10,000 miles per hour. After being weightless for nine minutes, Able and Baker returned to Earth in good condition. Their flight helped scientists learn even more about how space travel affects the body.

In 1961, the United States launched a chimp named Ham into space aboard a rocket. Ham had been trained to pull levers during the flight. This was an important step. Scientists learned that it was possible to perform tasks during a spaceflight. A few months after Ham's flight, the United States sent its first human astronaut, Alan Shepard, into space. The Soviet Union had already sent a man into space earlier that year. After more than ten dogs had been launched into space, Yuri Gagarin was the first human to orbit Earth.

Animal astronauts helped pave the way for human astronauts. Thanks to these animals, scientists learned that humans could survive space travel.

Read each sentence and check whether it gives the main idea of the passage or a supporting detail.

	Main Idea	Supporting Detail

1. A dog named Laika was the first living thing to orbit Earth.
2. The United States sent monkeys named Patricia and Mike into space.
3. Many animals traveled into space and paved the way for human astronauts.
4. Animal astronauts helped scientists learn how to send humans into space.
5. Two monkeys named Able and Baker traveled 10,000 miles per hour in a spaceship.
6. Animals helped scientists learn how space travel affects the body.
7. A chimp named Ham went into space and even pulled levers during flight.
8. Thanks to animals, scientists learned that humans could survive space travel.

Teamwork

All the girls on the soccer team gathered around Coach Lund and waited for the big announcement.

"I think everyone will agree that Kelly will be a great team captain this year," Coach Lund said. After the girls finished congratulating Kelly, Coach Lund handed her a shiny whistle she would use to help him run drills. She raced to the field to begin practice, smiling all the way.

As it turned out, helping the coach run practice drills was only one of Kelly's responsibilities. Kelly also had to call all the girls on the team and remind them about the games. If the time or location changed, Kelly had to make sure everyone knew. Organizing refreshments was also her responsibility. She filled the water jug and brought it to the field during practice. On game days a healthy snack needed to be provided for the team. It seemed like there was no end to the details.

At the team's third game of the season, Kelly felt like a zombie on the field. Her teammate Julie passed her the ball, but Kelly wasn't paying attention. The other team got control of the ball and made a goal.

"What happened out there?" Julie asked during the break. "I kicked the ball right to you, and it was like you didn't even see it!"

"I'm sorry," Kelly said. "I had just realized that I forgot to remind everyone about the team photo. And I forgot to put cups by the water jug! I lost my focus." Kelly felt like crying. This wasn't the first time she had gotten distracted during a game. She was always worrying instead of concentrating on her playing. She even worried that maybe she just wasn't a good enough leader to be the team captain.

"Playing your best and trying to win is more important than worrying about cups," Julie said. "My sister was team captain last year. She didn't try to do everything herself. The other girls on the team helped out a lot. You just have to ask."

Kelly knew Julie was right. She looked for ways the team could support her. Since all the girls on the team had e-mail, Julie agreed to send out reminders for the games over e-mail. Kelly also started a schedule to rotate who brought refreshments and cups. She still had to follow up on things, but she saved a lot of time by sharing the workload.

Now that she was less overwhelmed, Kelly could return her attention to her game. She led her team all the way to the championship, and she even remembered to bring cups and refreshments to the final game.

Decide if the sentence describes the story's setting, conflict, resolution, or theme. Connect each sentence with the correct word.

1. Kelly asks her teammates to share some of the workload, and her playing improves.

2. A good leader works hard but also isn't afraid to let others help.

3. The story takes place at soccer practice and soccer games.

4. Kelly finds her duties as team captain overwhelming and she loses focus while playing.

Setting

Conflict

Resolution

Theme

Summarize the plot of the story.

_____

_____

_____

_____

_____

_____

_____

_____

_____

Answer the questions.

1. Why was Kelly smiling after Coach Lund gave her the whistle?

    _____

    _____

2. What were some of Kelly's responsibilities as team captain?

    _____

    _____

3. What did Julie confront Kelly about during the break?

    _____

    _____

4. Why did Kelly lose focus while playing?

    _____

    _____

5. What advice did Julie give Kelly?

    _____

    _____

6. How did Kelly's teammates help share the workload?

    _____

    _____

7. After Kelly asked for help, how did things change?

    _____

    _____

8. What qualities do you think make a good leader?

    _____

    _____

A Letter from Philadelphia

As you read the passage, look for the underlined sentences.

If the statement is a fact, write an F in the box. If it's an opinion, write an O.

When I came to Philadelphia to visit Aunt Bonnie, I had no idea what a great city this is! I've only been here a few days, and already I've visited so many wonderful places. 1.☐ <u>Philadelphia is the best city on Earth!</u>

One of our first stops was a tour of Independence Hall. 2.☐ <u>This is where the Continental Congress met and signed the Declaration of Independence in 1776.</u> It all happened in the Assembly Room. The room looked small and simple, considering that fifty-six men were all packed in there during the hottest months of the summer. 3.☐ <u>Eleven years later, the United States Constitution was written in this very same building!</u> 4.☐ <u>It was really exciting to be in a place with so much history.</u>

We also went to see the Liberty Bell. Back in 1776, the bell rang to call people to Independence Square. 5.☐ <u>It was there that the Declaration of Independence was first read aloud to the public.</u> The bell started to crack many years ago, but people preserved it. 6.☐ <u>The line to see the Liberty Bell was too long, but it was worth it!</u>

The next day we went to visit Franklin Court. This area is named after Benjamin Franklin, and it has all sorts of great things to see. I explored the

underground museum and saw many of Franklin's inventions. 7.☐ The best part of the museum was an exhibit called the "Franklin Exchange." In this exhibit, I could pick up a phone and call someone that corresponded with Franklin. Then I could listen to their exchange. What a great way to learn about this amazing man!

Since Ben Franklin was a printer, Franklin Court also has a print shop. I learned all about the history of printing. 8.☐ Ben Franklin also helped start the U.S. postal service. At the museum about the history of the postal service, I saw mail pouches that were used on the Pony Express.

We also stopped at the Betsy Ross House. 9.☐ The story of Betsy Ross is very inspiring. She was a widow and she worked as a seamstress to support herself. She sewed the first American flag with white stars and red and white stripes. 10.☐ Congress adopted the flag on June 14, 1777, and this is why we celebrate Flag Day on that day. Her house is decorated to look just as it would have back in the 1770s. Seeing furniture from that period was really interesting.

I am having such a great time, I want to come back again next summer. There is so much to see and learn here, I'm sure I would never get bored. Seeing the places where important historic events happened really makes history come alive!

A Bump in the Road

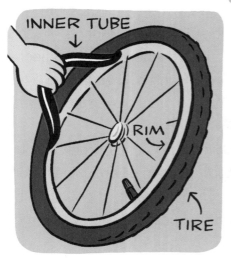

INNER TUBE

RIM

TIRE

You're riding your bike down a rocky lane, and suddenly your front wheel wobbles out of control. A small rock has pierced through the tire and made a hole. You've got a flat tire! Patching a hole in a bike tire is easy if you follow these simple steps.

The first step is to let the rest of the air out of the tire. Take off the valve cap and press down on the valve. You can now remove the deflated tire from the bike wheel. To do this, set the wheel on the floor. Grab the metal rim and pry the tire away from it.

As you separate the tire from the rim, you'll see a tube inside the tire. This is the "inner tube." You'll need to find where the hole is in the inner tube. First, remove the inner tube from the tire. To find the hole, put the whole tube underwater. Look for where the bubbles are coming out, and that's where the hole is.

Now it's time to patch the hole. Before you can put the patch on, the inner tube needs to be totally dry. Also, you need to roughen up the rubber on the inner tube. This will help the patch to stick better. Use sandpaper or a scraper, and rub the area around the hole. Make sure there is no dirt on the fresh rubber. Spread some glue around the hole, and then press the patch firmly on the tube. Let it dry for several minutes.

The tube is patched, and you can put your tire back together. Pump a little air back into the tube to give it a doughnut shape. Slide the inner tube back inside the tire. Then stretch the tire back over the metal rim. Your wheel is back to normal, and your bike is ready for another ride!

Find your way through the maze by connecting the events in the correct sequence.

START

Let the glue dry for several minutes.

Pry the tire away from the rim and remove the inner tube.

Put the inner tube underwater to find the hole.

Let the remaining air out of the tire.

Use sandpaper to roughen up the rubber around the hole.

Spread glue on the tire and press the patch on.

Slide the tube back inside the tire and put the tire on the wheel.

Look for bubbles coming from the hole in the tube.

FINISH

Amazing Atoms

Have you ever wondered how many times you could divide something in half? Let's say that you took an apple and cut it in half. Then you divided that half in two. You continued splitting each piece of the apple in half, over and over again. Would you ever get a piece that was so small it couldn't be divided?

As early as 400 BC a Greek thinker named Democritus asked this same question. Democritus gazed at a long stretch of beach and realized that it was made of countless grains of sand. Each grain of sand was tiny by itself, but millions of grains together formed a beach. He figured that all matter was made up of tiny, indestructable particles. He called these pieces *atomos*, which means "indivisible particle."

After Democritus died, it wasn't until the 1800s that scientists returned to his idea of small, indivisible particles. Around 1803, a schoolteacher and chemist named John Dalton brought back the idea that atoms were the basic building blocks of all matter. He explained that different types of matter were made up of different types of atoms. The atoms that make up a rock, for example, are different from the atoms that make up an apple. But all of the rock atoms are the same.

Another scientist built on this idea and started organizing the different atoms. Around 1869, Dmitri Mendeleev started putting atoms into groups of elements based on atomic weight. He made a table to show all the different types of elements.

At this point, scientists knew that atoms existed and they knew how to weigh them. Still, they didn't know what the inside of an atom actually looked like. Around 1911, a scientist named Ernest Rutherford figured out that there are tiny particles inside an atom. The very center of the atom is called the nucleus. Inside the nucleus there are small particles with a positive charge called protons. Orbiting around the nucleus are particles with a negative charge called electrons. Later, scientists learned that the nucleus also contained particles called neutrons, which have no charge.

Protons, neutrons, and electrons are very tiny and weigh very little. It would take 2.7 billion electrons to weigh as much as a penny. It has taken scientists many years and lots of experiments to answer the question that Democritus first asked thousands of years ago. As scientists continue to ask more questions, they discover even more about the atom!

Using the information from the passage, complete the diagram and the timeline below. Use the words in the box to label the diagram of the atom.

nucleus	proton	electron	orbit

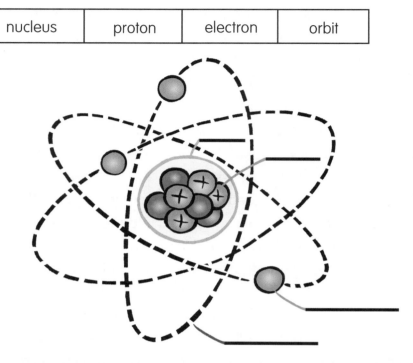

Now fill in the blanks with words from the box to complete the timeline.

weight	inside	atomos	matter

400 BC   Democritus said that _____ are tiny indestructible particles.

1803   John Dalton brought back the idea of atoms as basic building blocks of _____.

1869   Dmitri Mendeleev organized atoms according to _____.

1911   Ernest Rutherford figured out what the _____ of an atom looked like.

A **conclusion** is something that is not stated in the passage. You draw conclusions using clues from the text and your own logic.

1. Circle the most logical conclusion you can draw from the passage.
    a) As time passed, scientists got more and more confused about the atom.
    b) If scientists had worked harder, they would have discovered the atom earlier.
    c) Scientists built on each other's ideas to discover more about the atom.

2. Read the conclusion and circle the clues that support it. There may be more than one correct clue!
    Conclusion: At first, many people were not interested in the idea of the atom.
    Clues:
    a) After Democritus died, nobody studied the atom for over 2,000 years.
    b) Protons, neutrons, and electrons are tiny and do not weigh very much.
    c) It wasn't until 1803 that scientists starting thinking about the atom again.
    d) John Dalton was a schoolteacher and chemist.

3. Find clues from the reading passage that support the conclusion. List the facts on the lines below.
    Conclusion: The atom was not discovered by one person, but by many scientists over a long period of time.
    Clues: _____
    _____
    _____
    _____
    _____
    _____
    _____

Sequoyah

For many years, the people of the Cherokee tribe had no written language. They told stories to pass down their history, but they weren't able to record anything. A Cherokee man named Sequoyah helped change that. By inventing a written language, Sequoyah helped his Cherokee tribe preserve their culture.

Sequoyah had always been amazed by people who made marks on paper to communicate, a practice the natives called "talking leaves." Sequoyah served in the War of 1812, and he watched the American soldiers writing orders and letters. As the soldiers recorded the events of the war, Sequoyah realized that a writing system would help the Cherokee people record their own history. After the war, he dedicated his life to developing a written Cherokee language.

It took twelve years for Sequoyah to complete the writing system. When he first showed the alphabet to the chief leaders, they were upset. They believed that "talking leaves" were evil. Despite their reaction, Sequoyah's writing system spread quickly. The language was officially adopted by the tribe in 1825. Within a few years, the Bible had been translated into Cherokee along with many hymns. It only took about two weeks for someone who spoke Cherokee to learn Sequoyah's writing system. Thanks to his alphabet, thousands of Cherokee people could read and write their own language.

Sequoyah's writing system had a huge impact on the Cherokee tribe. They could now record their history and write letters and books. By 1828, the first Cherokee newspaper was printed, making it the first Native American newspaper published in the United States. Most importantly, the writing system allowed the tribe to create a written record of their culture. They could pass down their stories through storytelling and through writing.

Today, there is a National Park in California named after Sequoyah. The giant trees in the park are called Sequoyah trees, and they remind us of how he brought "talking leaves" to the Cherokee tribe.

Read each sentence and check whether it gives the main idea of the passage or a supporting detail.

	Main Idea	Supporting Detail
1. By inventing a written language, Sequoyah helped his Cherokee tribe preserve their culture.		
2. Thanks to Sequoyah, thousands of Cherokee people could read and write their language.		
3. During the War of 1812, Sequoyah watched American soldiers reading and writing.		
4. It took twelve years for Sequoyah to develop his writing system.		
5. Within a few years, the Bible had been translated into Cherokee along with many hymns.		
6. Sequoyah had a huge impact on the Cherokee tribe by creating a written Cherokee language.		
7. By 1828, the first Cherokee newspaper was printed, making it the first Native American newspaper published in the United States.		
8. The Sequoyah trees of Sequoyah National Park are named after Sequoyah.		

The Safe House

Leaves crunched under Martin's boots as he hiked through the woods in the darkness. He loved to walk through the woods that surrounded his family's plantation and look at the stars. When Martin reached the edge of his family's property, he paused. The woman who owned the house next door was hanging a lantern on the hitching post by her front door. He had watched her hang this lantern the past few nights when he was out on his walks. Martin wondered why she would leave a lantern outside her house. The woman lived alone and went to bed early. It didn't make sense.

As Martin sat down to tighten his boot laces, he heard rustling in the trees. Two shadows emerged from the woods and approached the woman's house. When they reached the front door, the light of the lantern revealed that they were actually slaves! They knocked on the door, and the woman quickly opened it and hustled them inside.

Martin had heard that there was an underground network of people who helped slaves escape to the free states or Canada. The slaves traveled by night and stopped at "safe houses" to rest. The lantern on the hitching post must have been the signal that the woman's house was a "safe house." Those slaves in the house were runaways, and she was helping them escape!

If Martin told anyone about what he saw, the slaves would be severely punished, perhaps even killed. The woman would be punished as well. Martin felt very confused. He had always felt that slavery was wrong and he understood why a slave would want to be free. Should he let them get away with it?

Suddenly dogs barked and men shouted through the woods. It was the slave hunters, and they were probably looking for the runaways Martin had just seen. As the group got closer, Martin saw the fierce look in the men's eyes and the dogs' sharp teeth. They seemed so cold and cruel.

The men spotted Martin and called out to him. "We're after two runaways, just turned up missing. Seen or heard anything out here, young man?"

Martin took a deep breath. "No," he said. "This is my family's plantation, and I walk these woods almost every night. Nothing unusual tonight."

"They must have gone the other way," the man said. He whistled to his dogs, and the group ran off in the opposite direction. Martin breathed a sigh of relief. He felt good about what he had done. He decided he wouldn't tell anyone about the safe house. In his own small way, he had helped a few slaves get a little closer to freedom.

Decide if the sentence describes the story's setting, conflict, resolution, or theme. Connect each sentence with the correct word.

1. Freedom is a right worth fighting and risking for.

2. When the slave hunters arrive, Martin decides not to turn in the runaways.

3. Martin wonders if he should turn in his neighbor and the runaway slaves.

4. The story takes place on a southern plantation before the Civil War.

Setting

Conflict

Resolution

Theme

Summarize the plot of the story.

_____

_____

_____

_____

_____

_____

_____

_____

_____

Answer the questions.

1. What did Martin notice when he was out on his nightly walk?

   _____

   _____

2. Why did Martin find the woman's behavior strange?

   _____

   _____

3. How did Martin figure out that the woman was helping runaways?

   _____

   _____

4. What is a "safe house"?

   _____

   _____

5. What would have happened if Martin had turned in the woman and the runaways?

   _____

   _____

6. How do you think Martin felt when he saw the slave hunters?

   _____

   _____

7. Why do you think Martin decided not to tell the slave hunters about the runaways?

   _____

   _____

8. How did Martin feel after he told the slave hunters there was nothing unusual?

   _____

   _____

The School Play

As you read the poster, look for the underlined sentences.
If the statement is a fact, write an F in the box.
If it's an opinion, write an O.

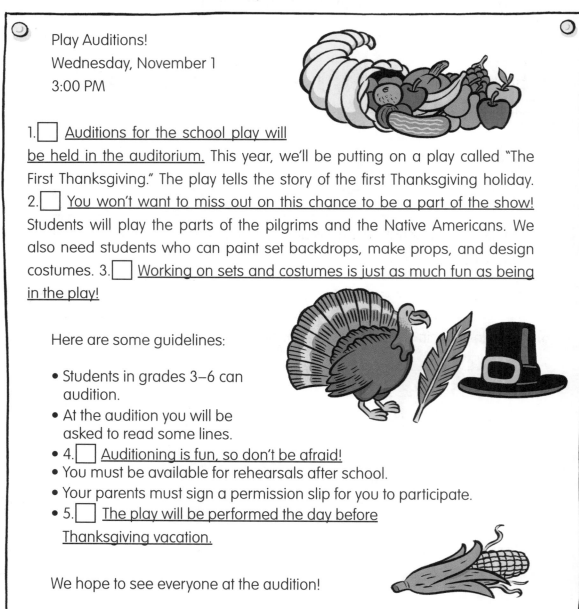

Play Auditions!
Wednesday, November 1
3:00 PM

1. ☐ <u>Auditions for the school play will be held in the auditorium.</u> This year, we'll be putting on a play called "The First Thanksgiving." The play tells the story of the first Thanksgiving holiday.
2. ☐ <u>You won't want to miss out on this chance to be a part of the show!</u> Students will play the parts of the pilgrims and the Native Americans. We also need students who can paint set backdrops, make props, and design costumes. 3. ☐ <u>Working on sets and costumes is just as much fun as being in the play!</u>

Here are some guidelines:

- Students in grades 3–6 can audition.
- At the audition you will be asked to read some lines.
- 4. ☐ <u>Auditioning is fun, so don't be afraid!</u>
- You must be available for rehearsals after school.
- Your parents must sign a permission slip for you to participate.
- 5. ☐ <u>The play will be performed the day before Thanksgiving vacation.</u>

We hope to see everyone at the audition!

Eastshore Elementary School presents
"The First Thanksgiving"
3:30 PM, November 23

All students are invited to attend this year's school play, "The First Thanksgiving." 6.☐ <u>Students have been rehearsing after school all month long.</u> You'll learn about American history as you watch the story unfold. It's important to support your friends who have worked so hard to put the show together. 7.☐ <u>Seeing the play is the best way to start your Thanksgiving vacation!</u>

Tickets are free!
8.☐ <u>No food is allowed in the auditorium.</u>
The play starts at 3:30, and no latecomers will be admitted.
9.☐ <u>Both young children and adults will enjoy it, so invite your families!</u>
The play lasts for about an hour.
10.☐ <u>The refreshments served after the play will be delicious.</u>

Using Your Imagination

To be a good reader, it is important to understand the role of setting, conflict, resolution, and theme in a story. Use your imagination and fill in the lines below with details for your own story.

Setting: _____

_____

_____

_____

Conflict: _____

_____

_____

_____

Resolution: _____

_____

_____

_____

_____

Theme: _____

_____

_____

_____

**Use the information on page 60 to write
your very own story!**

_____

_____

_____

_____

_____

_____

_____

_____

_____

_____

_____

_____

_____

_____

_____

_____

_____

_____

Answer Key

Page 5

START

FINISH

The correct path out of the maze connects the following sentences in this order:
1) The Wheatley family purchased Phillis from a slave trade ship in Boston.
2) The Wheatleys helped Phillis learn to read and write.
3) Phillis's poem about a Boston preacher became popular.
4) A book of 39 of Phillis's poems was published.
5) After her death, people continued to publish the letters and poems.

Page 8

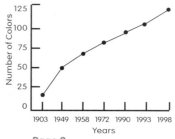

Page 9
1. a
2. b, d
3. Answers will vary
   Kids spend 3 hours a week coloring with crayons.
   At the age of 10, most kids have used 730 crayons.
   Crayola makes 3 million crayons a year.
   Crayons are available in 80 countries.

Page 11
1. Detail
2. Detail
3. Main Idea
4. Detail
5. Detail
6. Detail
7. Main Idea
8. Main Idea

Page 14
1. Resolution
2. Setting
3. Conflict
4. Theme
Answers will vary.

Page 15
Answers will vary.
1. Gabe was upset that they would have to give Tracer back to the dog school.
2. They taught him to be confident and friendly and to follow voice commands.
3. He felt angry that Tracer was going to live with someone else.
4. After meeting Tracer's new owner, Gabe felt proud of Tracer and glad that he could help train him.
5. Tracer's owner thanked Gabe for training the dog and said he could visit Tracer.
6. Gabe realized that Tracer was going to a good home where he would be needed.
7. Answers will vary.
8. Answers will vary.

Pages 16-17
1. O
2. F
3. O
4. F
5. O
6. F
7. F
8. F
9. O
10. F

Page 19
The correct path out of the maze connects the following sentences in this order:

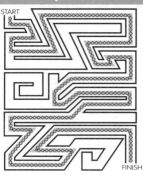

START

FINISH

1) You sit on your foot and place too much pressure on it.
2) The pressure blocks the pathway from your foot to your brain.
3) Nerves cannot send or receive messages from the brain.
4) Your foot starts to tingle, so you change positions.
5) The nerves slowly "wake up" and start to flow again.

Page 22

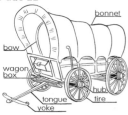

bonnet
bow
wagon box
tongue
yoke
hub
tire

Page 23
1. c
2. a, d
3. Answers will vary.
   The floor sloped to keep objects from rolling out.
   Side boards were slanted to keep water out.
   The wood planks could be made water-tight and float down a river.
   The bonnet made a roof to protect from the wind and sun.

Page 25
1. Detail
2. Detail
3. Main Idea

4. Detail
5. Main Idea
6. Main Idea
7. Detail
8. Detail

Page 28
1. Setting
2. Resolution
3. Theme
4. Conflict
Answers will vary.

Page 29
Answers will vary.
1. His father was getting old and wanted to see his sons.
2. He was not good at reading maps.
3. He met birds, crickets, and the djinn spirits.
4. The birds helped him sort his maps, the crickets directed him to the island of the djiins, and the djinns told Sadaka his brothers were on the island of Pemba.
5. Sadaka had to sort bags of seeds, chop down a tree with one stroke, and find the Sultan's favorite daughter at the ball.
6. The birds helped him sort the seeds, the djinns helped him cut the tree, and the crickets told him which daughter was the Sultan's favorite.
7. Sadaka's brothers were thrown in jail because they were rude.
8. Yes, Sadaka leaves home for a task, gets help from three friends, and must face a villain and pass a test.

Pages 30-31
1. F
2. O
3. O
4. O
5. F
6. O
7. O
8. F
9. O
10. F

Answer Key

Page 33

START

FINISH

The correct path out of the maze connects the following sentences in this order:

1) At 17, Marco left on a journey with his father and uncle.
2) Marco reached China and lived there for 17 years.
3) When he returned to Venice, Marco told stories about his travels.
4) Marco passed time in prison by telling stories of his adventures.
5) A book about Marco's travels was published.

Page 36

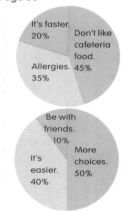

It's faster. 20%

Don't like cafeteria food. 45%

Allergies. 35%

Be with friends. 10%

It's easier. 40%

More choices. 50%

Page 37

1. b
2. c, d
3. Answers will vary.
   45% of students said they didn't like the taste.
   But 40% of the students still buy their lunch.

One student said the cafeteria food didn't taste good. Another student said cafeteria food tasted fresher.

Page 39

1. Detail
2. Detail
3. Main Idea
4. Main Idea
5. Detail
6. Detail
7. Detail
8. Main Idea

Page 42

1. Resolution
2. Theme
3. Setting
4. Conflict
Answers will vary.

Page 43

Answers will vary.

1. She was excited about being the new team captain.
2. She had to run practice drills, remind players about the game, organize refreshments, and bring the water jug and cups.
3. Julie wanted to know why Kelly had missed a pass on the field.
4. She was worrying about the team photo and water cups.
5. Julie explained that when her sister was team captain, she asked the team members to help with the workload.
6. Julie sent out reminder e-mails for the game, and they rotated the refreshments.
7. Kelly was able to focus on her playing again.
8. Answers will vary.

Pages 44-45

1. O
2. F
3. F
4. O
5. F
6. O
7. O
8. F
9. O
10. F

Page 47

START

FINISH

The correct path out of the maze connects the following sentences in this order:

1) Pry the tire away from the rim and remove the inner tube.
2) Put the inner tube underwater to find the hole.
3) Use sandpaper to roughen up the rubber around the hole.
4) Spread glue on the tire and press the patch on.
5) Slide the tube back inside the tire and put the tire on the wheel.

Page 50

nucleus
proton
electron
orbit

— 400 BC Democritus said that <u>atomos</u> are tiny indestructible particles.

— 1803 John Dalton brought back the idea of atoms as basic building blocks of <u>matter</u>.

— 1869 Dimitri Mendeleev organized atoms according to <u>weight</u>.

— 1911 Ernest Rutherford figured out what the <u>inside</u> of an atom looked like.

Page 51

1. c
2. a, c
3. Answers will vary.
   Many different scientists, including Democritus, John Dalton, Mendeleev, and Rutherford helped learn about the atom bit by bit.

Page 53

1. Main Idea
2. Main Idea
3. Detail
4. Detail
5. Detail
6. Main Idea
7. Detail
8. Detail

Page 56

1. Theme
2. Resolution
3. Conflict
4. Setting
Answers will vary.

Page 57

Answers will vary.

1. His neighbor was hanging a lantern from a hitching post.
2. She lived alone and went to bed early, so there was no need for a lantern.
3. He saw two slaves go inside her house.
4. A "safe house" is a house where runaway slaves could rest as they made the journey to the free states.
5. The slaves and the woman would have been punished severely.
6. He probably felt scared and it made him sad that they would hurt the slaves so badly.
7. Answers will vary.
8. He felt glad that he had helped the slaves get closer to freedom.

Pages 58-59

1. F
2. O
3. O
4. O
5. F
6. F
7. O
8. F
9. O
10. O

Pages 60-61

Answers will vary.

Nice work!

_____,

(Name)

you're a
reading
champion!